klick kliiick

Published by Sourcebooks eXplore, an imprint of Sourcebooks Kids
P.O. Box 4410, Naperville, Illinois 60567-4410
(630) 961-3900
sourcebookskids.com

Cataloging-in-Publication Data is on file with the Library of Congress.

Source of Production: Wing King Tong Paper Products Co. Ltd., Shenzhen, Guangdong Province, China
Date of Production: April 2024
Run Number: 5038572

Printed and bound in China.
WKT 10 9 8 7 6 5 4 3 2 1

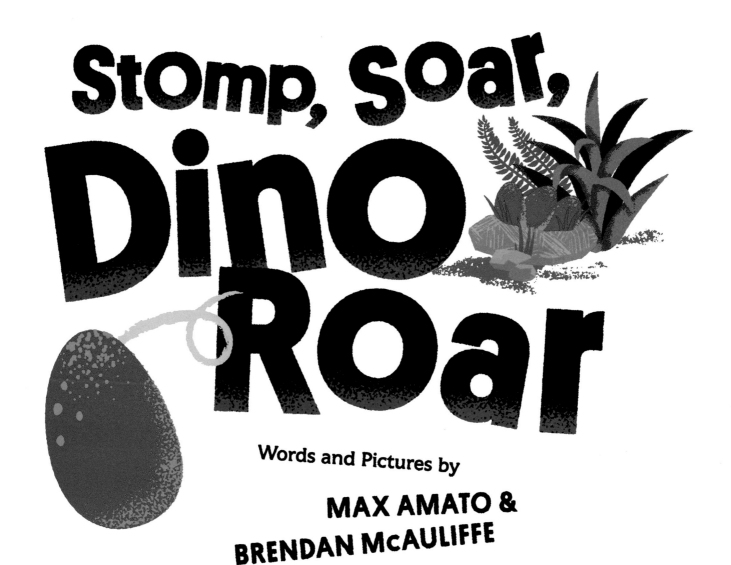

Stomp, Soar, Dino Roar

Words and Pictures by

MAX AMATO &
BRENDAN McAULIFFE

sourcebooks
eXplore

shhheka

shekaaa

craaack

blink
blink

shkradack

This is Terri.

Terri is a *Triceratops*, and this is Terri's world.
(try-SAIR-uh-tops)
There are crawling critters and shaking trees, scorching volcanoes
and stormy seas, smelly bogs and bitter leaves, and most of all…
there are sounds.

Sounds shriek in the air

kerr kaaaw

kaaaw kerrr

and slither on the ground.

hissssss hisssss

Sounds flitter close by.

phit
phit
phit
phit
phit

But how does
Terri sound?

Wait! That isn't Terri.
That's a *Saurolophus* yowling
(SOR-uh-loaf-us)

and *Velociraptors* prowling.
(vuh-LOSS-uh-rap-turs)

A *Plesiosaurus* dunking
(plee-see-uh-SOR-us)

flap

flaaap

flap

flaaap

and *Pteranodons* hunting.
(tuh-RA-nuh-daans)
But how does
Terri sound?

That's not Terri.
Those are *Pachycephalosauruses* dueling
(pack-uh-SEF-uh-luh-SOR-us-es)

pitter patter

pitter patter

pitter patter

and *Corythoraptors* fooling.
(koh-RITH-uh-rap-turs)

An *Edmontosaurus* splashing

(ed-mon-tuh-SOR-us)

and an *Ankylosaurus* thrashing.
(ang-kuh-low-SOR-us)

Those are dragonflies swarming

bOhm bOhm

and a *Titanosaurus* performing.
(tie-tan-uh-SOR-us)
But how does Terri sound?

Okay, that's definitely not Terri.
What is that *crunch, crunch*?

Oh no!
A *Tyrannosaurus* looking for its lunch!
(tuh-ran-uh-SOR-us)

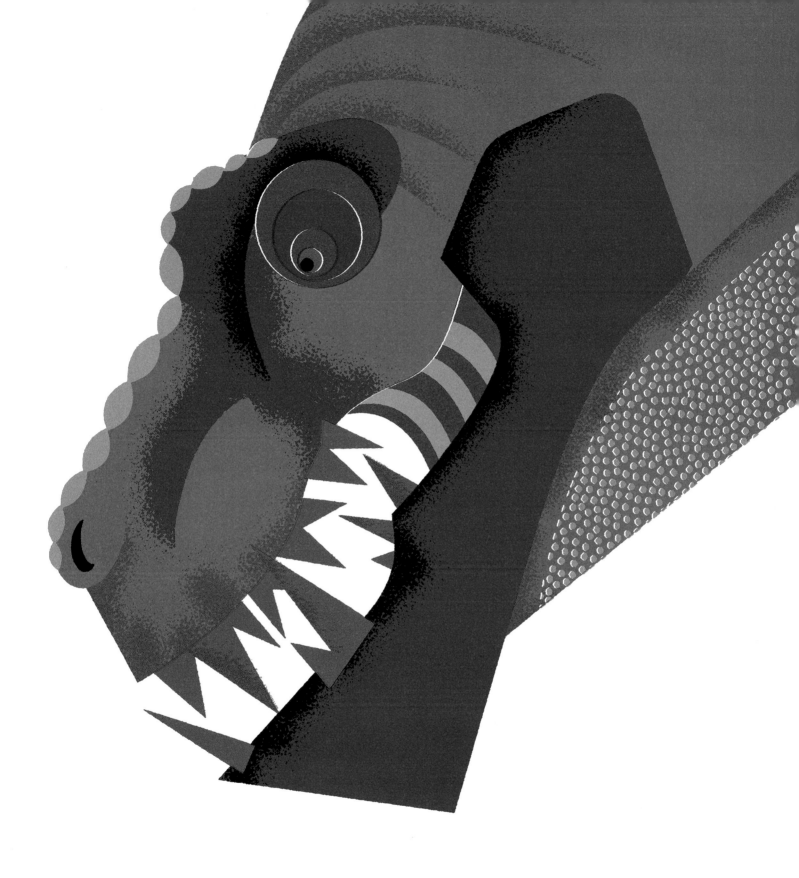

Don't. Make. A sound.

meep

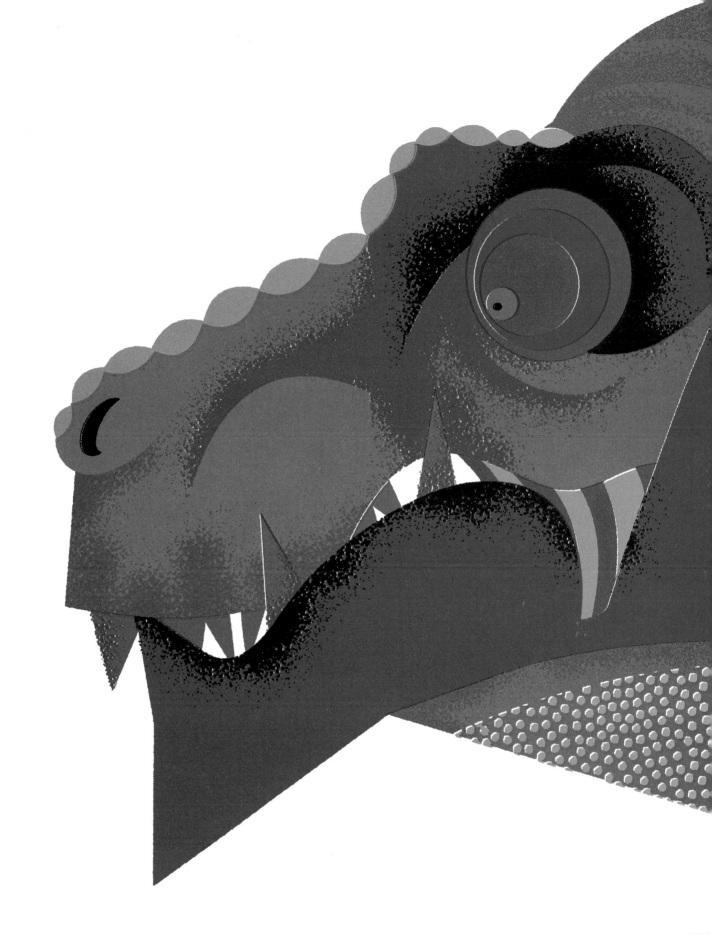

This is Terri's world.
It's full of sounds...
including hers.

Dino Details

All of these dates, measurements, and facts are approximate based on the current science. We're always learning new things. Isn't that cool?!

ANKYLOSAURUS
(ang-kuh-low-SOR-us)

Name Meaning: Fused or bent lizard
Age: 70–66 million years ago · **Weight:** 8,000–18,000 lbs
Length: About 26 feet · **Location:** North America
Description: A large, heavily armored herbivore (plant eater) known for its beak and the bony club at the end of its tail used for protection from predators.

6 Feet

PACHYCEPHALOSAURUS
(pack-uh-SEF-uh-luh-SOR-us)

Name Meaning: Thick-headed lizard
Age: 100–66 million years ago · **Weight:** 2,200 lbs
Length: About 15 feet · **Location:** North America
Description: A thick-skulled herbivore thought to have battled its own species by ramming headfirst.

PLESIOSAURUS
(plee-see-uh-SOR-us)

Name Meaning: Near lizard · **Age:** 215–66 million years ago
Weight: 150–100,000 lbs · **Length:** 15–50 feet
Location: Seas around Asia, Europe, Australia, North America
Description: A marine carnivore (meat eater) known for its long neck, small head, and all four limbs shaped like paddles for swimming.

TITANOSAURUS
(tie-tan-uh-SOR-us)

Name Meaning: Titanic lizard
Age: 163.5–66 million years ago · **Weight:** 23,000–130,000 lbs
Length: 23–85 feet · **Location:** India
Description: A massive herbivore characterized by its long neck and tail, this diverse group had some of the largest known land animals, some even nearing the size of whales.

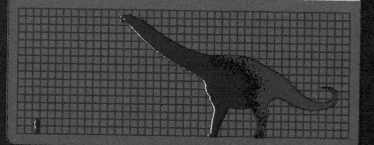

TRICERATOPS
(try-SAIR-uh-tops)

Name Meaning: Three-horned face
Age: 68–66 million years ago · **Weight:** 12,100 lbs
Length: 26–30 feet · **Location:** North America
Description: A beaked herbivore with a bony neck frill and three horns, making its massive skull roughly one third the size of its body.

Terri

CORYTHORAPTOR
(koh-RITH-uh-rap-tur)

Name Meaning: Helmeted thief
Age: 72–66 million years ago · **Weight:** 84 lbs
Length: Over 5 feet · **Location:** South China
Description: A birdlike herbivore with a large beak that connected to a head crest and long feathers on both its arms and tail.

EDMONTOSAURUS
(ed-mon-tuh-SOR-us)

Name Meaning: Edmonton lizard · **Age:** 76–66 million years ago
Weight: 7,500 lbs · **Length:** Around 30–40 feet
Location: North America
Description: A coastal herbivore that could move on either hind legs or all fours, equipped with one thousand teeth designed to grind pine needles, pine cones, and twigs.

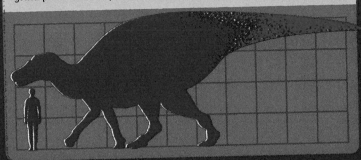

PTERANODON
(tuh-RA-nuh-daan)

Name Meaning: Winged and toothless
Age: 74–70 million years ago · **Weight:** 55–110 lbs
Wingspan: Up to 25 feet
Location: North America, Europe, South America, Asia
Description: A flying carnivore with a large bony head crest on the skull and a leathery wings.

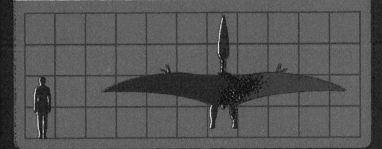

SAUROLOPHUS
(SOR-uh-loaf-us)

Name Meaning: Ridged lizard · **Age:** 74–70 million years ago
Weight: 4,200 lbs · **Length:** 30 feet
Location: Canada, Mongolia
Description: A duck-billed herbivore characterized by a spikelike head crest most likely used to control its body temperature or breathing.

TYRANNOSAURUS
(tuh-ran-uh-SOR-us)

Name Meaning: Tyrant lizard
Age: 150–66 million years ago · **Weight:** 15,400 lbs
Length: 46 feet · **Location:** North America
Description: A predatory carnivore, known to have walked on powerful hind legs, with adults boasting around sixty teeth.

VELOCIRAPTOR
(vuh-LOSS-uh-rap-tur)

Name Meaning: Quick plunderer
Age: 74–70 million years ago · **Weight:** 15–100 lbs
Length: 6 feet · **Location:** Mongolia
Description: A feathered, fleet-footed carnivore known for its long head and large sickle-shaped claws on each foot.

Sonic Science

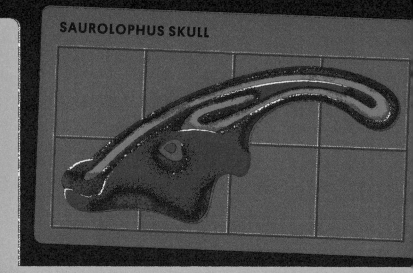

Dinosaurs existed millions of years before humans ever walked the Earth. This means we most likely will never know for certain what they sounded like. But we do know that animals of all shapes and sizes—and from all time periods—have used sound to talk to one another. By studying the structure and fossil records of dinosaurs' ears and heads, we can begin to understand the types of frequencies and sounds they were capable of hearing and making. For example, the *Saurolophus* had a unique, hollow head crest connected to their nose and throat that could have made an eerie howling noise.

Another way to guess what dinosaurs sounded like is by studying their living relatives. Many animals roaming today are descendants of prehistoric creatures. By listening to their sounds, we can begin to hear their predecessors. For example, scientists turn to modern birds like cassowaries to understand that *Velociraptors* may have made rumbling hums, murmurs, and percussive squawks. Or we can look to crocodilians, who share common ancestors with the *Tyrannosaurus*, to conclude the *Tyrannosaurus* most likely made a low-pitched bellow.

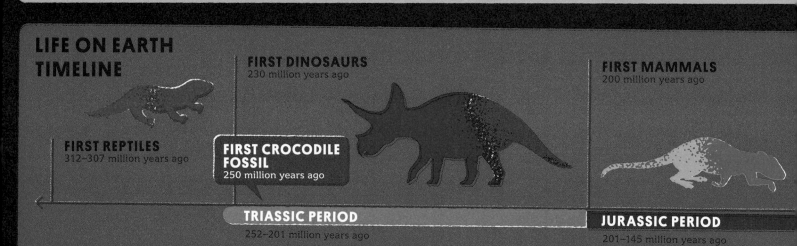

LIFE ON EARTH TIMELINE

FIRST DINOSAURS
230 million years ago

FIRST MAMMALS
200 million years ago

FIRST REPTILES
312–307 million years ago

FIRST CROCODILE FOSSIL
250 million years ago

TRIASSIC PERIOD
252–201 million years ago

JURASSIC PERIOD
201–145 million years ago

Terri's World

Terri was not a real dinosaur (but I'm sure you already knew that). If she were, she would have lived a long time ago. A *very* long time ago. So long ago that there was no ice on the planet. The rainforests extended to the North and South Poles. The seas were higher than they are today. The continents were slowly shifting and separating. Entire species of marine and land animals lived, evolved, and ceased to exist. We call this time the Cretaceous Period. This was the last of three periods in the Mesozoic Era, when dinosaurs ruled the Earth.

Approximately sixty-six million years ago, the world abruptly changed forever. There are many theories as to exactly what happened, but the most common one says that an asteroid the size of Mount Everest collided with Earth. Tsunamis and earthquakes damaged the landscape, and dust clouds blocked the Sun, wiping out three quarters of all plant and animal life. The lone survivors on land were small mammals and birds, creatures able to persevere despite the scarcity of vegetation and other sources of food. Over time these animals evolved and flourished, new plant life emerged from the rubble, and the lush planet that we know today came to be.

FIRST BIRDS
150 million years ago

FIRST FLOWERS
140–130 million ago

TERRI
68 million
years ago

PALEOGENE EXTINCTION EVENT
66 million years ago

FIRST HUMANS
2 million years ago

CRETACEOUS PERIOD
145–66 million years ago

TODAY